The Best
CHOCOLATE
DESSERTS

The Best
CHOCOLATE
DESSERTS

Cakes, Cookies, Brownies,
and Other Sinful Sweets

By Gregg R. Gillespie

BLACK DOG
& LEVENTHAL
PUBLISHERS
NEW YORK

Published by
Black Dog & Leventhal Publishers, Inc.
151 West 19th Street
New York, NY 10011

Distributed by
Workman Publishing
708 Broadway
New York, NY 10003

Manufactured in Spain

ISBN 1-57912-292-2

Library of Congress Cataloging-in-Publication Data is on file and available
from Black Dog & Leventhal Publishers, Inc.

Cover and interior design by 27.12 Design, Ltd.
Interior layout by Cindy Joy
Photography by Peter Barry

g f e d c b a

CONTENTS

BAKED FUDGE CAKE

makes 12 to 15 servings

4 oz. unsweetened chocolate, grated or finely chopped
⅓ cup butter or margarine
2 large eggs
1 cup granulated sugar
½ cup all-purpose flour

½ cup chopped walnuts
1 tsp. chocolate or vanilla extract
Pinch of salt
1½ to 2 cups chocolate fudge frosting

1. Position a rack in the center of the oven and preheat the oven to 350 degrees. Lightly grease a 13 by 9-inch pan. Line the bottom of the pan with greased waxed paper.
2. In the top of a double boiler, over simmering water, melt the chocolate and butter, stirring until smooth. Remove from heat.
3. In a large bowl, using an electric mixer on high speed, beat the eggs until thick and light-colored. Beat in the sugar. Beat in the chocolate mixture. Stir in the flour, walnuts, chocolate extract, and salt. Pour the mixture into the prepared pan and spread evenly.
4. Bake for 20 to 25 minutes, or until a cake tester inserted into the center comes out clean. Cool in the pan on a wire rack for 10 minutes. Invert onto a platter to cool completely.
5. Spread the frosting over the top and sides of the cake.

CHOCOLATE
CHOCOLATE TORTE
makes 10 to 12 servings

cake
8 oz. semi-sweet chocolate,
   grated or finely chopped
1½ tbsp. butter or margarine
5 large eggs
¼ cup granulated sugar
⅓ cup dark corn syrup

topping
¾ cup heavy cream
8 oz. semi-sweet chocolate,
   grated or finely chopped
1½ tbsp. butter or margarine,
   at room temperature
1½ tbsp. dark corn syrup
orange slices for garnish

1. Position a rack in the center of the oven and preheat the oven to
   350 degrees. Grease and flour a 9-inch round cake pan and line the
   bottom with waxed or parchment paper. Grease and flour the paper.
2. In the top of a double boiler over simmering water, melt the
   chocolate and butter, stirring until smooth. Remove from the heat.
3. In a large bowl, using an electric mixer on high speed, beat the eggs
   and sugar until thick and light-colored. Beat in the corn syrup.
   Pouring it in a thin stream, beat in the chocolate mixture on low
   speed. Pour the mixture into the prepared pan and spread evenly.
4. Bake for 1 hour, or until a cake tester inserted into the center comes
   out clean. Cool in the pan on a wire rack. Invert onto a serving plate.
5. To make the glaze, in a saucepan over low heat, warm the cream for 1
   minute. Reduce the heat and add the chocolate. Stir constantly until the
   chocolate is melted and the mixture is smooth. Remove from the heat.
   Let stand just until cool. Using a wire whisk, beat in the butter and corn
   syrup. Spread the glaze over the torte and garnish with orange slices.

GRASSHOPPER CHEESECAKE

makes 12 servings

crust
1½ cups chocolate wafer
  cookie crumbs
1 tbsp. granulated sugar
2 tbsp. butter or
  margarine, melted
filling
16 oz. cream cheese,
  at room temperature

1 cup granulated sugar
3 large eggs
¼ cup green crème de menthe
2 tbsp. crème de cacao
topping
3 oz. semi-sweet chocolate,
  grated or finely chopped
½ cup sour cream or yogurt

1. Position a rack in the center of the oven and preheat the oven to
   350 degrees. Lightly grease an 8-inch springform pan.
2. To make the crust, in a small bowl, combine the cookie crumbs,
   sugar, and the melted butter. Press firmly onto the bottom and up to
   an inch on the sides of the prepared pan. Chill.
3. To make the filling, in a large bowl, using an electric mixer on medium
   speed, beat the cream cheese and sugar until smooth. Beat in the
   eggs. Continue beating until the mixture is very smooth. Stir in the
   crème de menthe and crème de cacao. Pour into the chilled crust.
4. Bake for 35 to 40 minutes, or until a cake tester inserted into the
   center comes out clean. Cool in the pan on a wire rack.
5. To make the topping, melt the chocolate. Remove from the heat and
   cool slightly. Stir in the sour cream. Spread over the top of the cooled
   cheesecake. Chill 30 minutes, or until serving.
6. Remove the side of the pan and place the cheesecake on a serving plate.

FAST `N´ EASY
CHOCOLATE SHEET CAKE
makes 12 servings

1 package (3.4 oz.)
  cook-and-serve chocolate
  pudding mix
1 box (18.5 oz.) chocolate
  cake mix

2 cups semi-sweet
  chocolate chips
1 cup chopped walnuts,
  for garnish

1. Position a rack in the center of the oven and preheat the oven
    to 350 degrees. Lightly grease an 11½ by 17½-inch sheet pan.
    Line the pan with waxed or parchment paper and grease the paper.
2. Make the pudding mix according to the package directions and pour
    into a large mixing bowl. Gradually blend in the cake mix. Pour the
    mixture into the prepared pan and spread evenly. Sprinkle the
    chocolate chips over the top.
3. Bake for 30 to 35 minutes, or until a cake tester inserted into the
    center comes out clean. Spread the melted chocolate chips evenly
    over the top of the cake and sprinkle the walnuts on top. Cool in the
    pan on a wire rack. Invert cake onto the rack to cool completely.
    Cut into squares.

GOOD GUYS'
CHOCOLATE CAKE

makes 12 to 15 servings

2½ cups all-purpose flour
1 tsp. baking soda
Pinch of salt
4 oz. unsweetened chocolate,
   grated or finely chopped
½ cup water
2 cups granulated sugar
1 cup vegetable shortening

4 large eggs
1 cup buttermilk
1 tsp. vanilla extract
1¼ cups warm chocolate syrup
2 cups whipped topping
   for garnish
3 candy bars (8 oz. each),
   crushed, for garnish

1. Position a rack in the center of the oven and preheat the oven
   to 350 degrees. Lightly grease and flour a 13 by 9-inch pan.
2. Combine the flour, baking soda, and salt.
3. In the top of a double boiler over simmering water, combine the
   chocolate and water, stirring until smooth.
4. In a large bowl, using an electric mixer on medium speed, beat the
   shortening and sugar until fluffy. Beat in the eggs, one at a time.
   Beat in the buttermilk and vanilla extract. Pouring it in a thin stream,
   beat in the chocolate mixture. Gradually blend in the dry ingredients.
   Pour the mixture into the prepared pan and spread evenly.
5. Bake for 30 to 35 minutes, or until a cake tester inserted into the
   center comes out clean. Cool in the pan on a wire rack for 10
   minutes. Using a large fork, poke holes 1½ inches apart all over the
   top of the cake. Pour the chocolate syrup over the warm cake and
   cool completely. Chill for 30 minutes before serving.
6. To serve, spread the whipped topping over the top of the cake and
   sprinkle with the crushed candy bars.

PISTACHIO PUDDING
CHOCOLATE CAKE

makes 12 to 14 servings

½ cup chopped pistachios
1 box (18.5 oz.) yellow
  cake mix
1 package (3.4 oz.) pistachio
  instant pudding mix
1 cup canola oil

½ cup orange juice
3 large eggs
½ cup club soda
¾ cup chocolate syrup
Powdered sugar for garnish

1. Position a rack in the center of the oven and preheat the oven to 350 degrees. Lightly grease and flour a 10-inch Bundt pan. Sprinkle the pistachio nuts evenly over the bottom of the prepared pan.
2. In a large bowl, using an electric mixer on medium speed, beat the cake mix, pudding mix, oil, orange juice, eggs, and club soda until blended. Pour half of the mixture into the prepared pan, being careful not to disturb the pistachio nuts.
3. Add the chocolate syrup to the remaining batter and stir until well blended. Pour over the top of the mixture in the pan. Using a knife, swirl the batters two or three times. Do not overmix or touch the bottom or sides of the pan.
4. Bake for 40 to 45 minutes, or until a cake tester inserted into a light section of the cake comes out clean. Cool in the pan on a wire rack for 15 minutes. Invert onto the rack to cool completely. Place on a serving plate. Sprinkle with powdered sugar.

RED DEVIL´S FOOD CAKE

makes 12 servings

2 cups cake flour
1 tsp. baking soda
¼ tsp. salt
2 oz. semi-sweet chocolate, grated or finely chopped
½ cup butter or margarine

1½ cups granulated sugar
2 large eggs
1 tsp. vanilla extract
½ cup buttermilk
½ cup boiling water
1 tbsp. cocoa powder

1. Position a rack in the center of the oven and preheat the oven to 350 degrees. Lightly grease two 8-inch round cake pans. Line the bottoms with waxed or parchment paper. Butter the paper and flour the pans.
2. Combine and sift the flour, baking soda, and salt.
3. In the top of a double boiler over simmering water, combine the chocolate and butter, stirring until chocolate is melted and the mixture is smooth. Remove from the heat and stir in the sugar.
4. In a large bowl, using an electric mixer on medium speed, beat the eggs until thick and light-colored. Pouring it in a thin stream, beat in the chocolate mixture. Beat in the vanilla extract. Combine the buttermilk and boiling water. In three additions, blend in the dry ingredients, alternating with the buttermilk mixture, beginning and ending with the dry ingredients. Beat until well blended. The batter will be thin. Pour into the prepared pans and spread evenly.
5. Bake for 25 to 30 minutes, or until a cake tester inserted into the center comes out clean. Cool for 5 minutes in the pans on wire racks. Invert onto the racks to cool completely.
6. Sprinkle with cocoa powder.

TUNNEL OF FUDGE
CAKE

makes 16 servings

2½ cups chocolate frosting mix
2 cups all-purpose flour
2 cups walnuts, finely chopped
1½ cups butter or margarine,
  at room temperature
1½ cups granulated sugar
6 large eggs
Powdered sugar for garnish

1. Position a rack in the center of the oven and preheat the oven to 350 degrees. Grease and flour a 10-inch Bundt pan.
2. Combine the frosting mix, flour, and walnuts.
3. In a large bowl, using an electric mixer on medium speed, beat the butter and sugar until light and fluffy. Beat in the eggs, one at a time, beating until smooth and light-colored. Gradually blend in the dry ingredients. Pour the mixture into the prepared pan and spread evenly.
4. Bake for 55 to 60 minutes, or until the cake pulls from the sides of the pan. The cake will appear soft in the center. Cool in the pan on a wire rack for at least 1 hour.
5. Invert the cake onto a serving plate. Sprinkle the top of the cake with powdered sugar.

ALMOND
BRITTLE

makes 1½ to 2 pounds

2 cups granulated sugar
⅔ cup water
⅓ cup light corn syrup
¼ cup butter or margarine
½ cup unsweetened chocolate,
   grated or finely chopped

1 tsp. chocolate extract
½ tsp. baking soda
1½ cups almonds,
   coarsely chopped

1. Grease 15½ by 10½-inch jelly-roll pan.
2. In a saucepan, over medium heat, combine the sugar, water,
   corn syrup, and butter. Insert a candy thermometer and cook,
   without stirring, until 300 degrees. Remove from the heat. Quickly
   stir in the chocolate, chocolate extract, baking soda, and almonds.
   Pour the mixture onto the prepared pan and spread it out to the sides
   of the pan. Cool in the pan until hard. Break into pieces.

Baking note: The secret of this recipe is to spread the brittle very thinly.

CHOCOLATE-COVERED
BANANAS
makes 12 servings

6 medium bananas
1 cup semi-sweet
  chocolate chips

2 tbsp. butter or margarine
12 wooden Popsicle™ sticks
½ cup pecans, finely chopped

1. Peel the bananas and cut in half. Insert a wooden stick into the small
   end and place on a waxed paper-lined baking sheet. Freeze for 2 to 3
   hours, or until hard.
2. In the top of a double boiler over simmering water, melt the
   chocolate chips and butter, stirring until smooth.
3. Dip the frozen bananas into the chocolate and roll in the pecans.
   Freeze until the chocolate is hard. Serve or wrap in plastic wrap and
   freeze until serving.

CHOCOLATE COVERED CHERRIES

makes 10 to 15 cherries

1 jar (8 oz.) maraschino
   cherries with stems, drained
½ cup fresh orange juice,
   strained

1 tsp. maraschino liqueur
3 oz. semi-sweet chocolate,
   grated or finely chopped

1. Place the cherries in a small bowl. Add the orange juice and liqueur. Let stand for 30 minutes. Cover and freeze for 1 hour.
2. Melt the chocolate. Remove from the heat.
3. Drain the frozen cherries and wipe dry with paper towels. Dip the frozen cherries in the chocolate. Place each cherry on a waxed paper-lined baking sheet. Let stand at room temperature until firm. Place in the refrigerator until hard.

Baking note: Any kind of liqueur can be used in place of the maraschino liqueur. Coating chocolate may also be used in place of the semi-sweet chocolate listed above.

CHOCOLATE FUDGE
WITH CHERRIES

makes 1½ pounds

2 cups granulated sugar
1 cup milk
½ tsp. salt
2 oz. unsweetened chocolate, grated or finely chopped

2 tbsp. butter or margarine
1 tsp. crème de cacao
½ cup walnuts, chopped
¼ cup candied cherries, finely chopped

1. Lightly grease a 13 by 9-inch pan.
2. In a saucepan over low heat, combine the sugar, milk, and salt, stirring until blended. Stir in the chocolate. Bring to a boil, stirring occasionally. Insert a candy thermometer and cook until 234 degrees. Remove from the heat and stir in the butter. Cool to 130 degrees.
3. Stir in the crème de cacao. Return to the heat and cook over medium heat until the mixture starts to thicken. Remove from the heat and cool. Fold in the walnuts and cherries. Immediately pour into the prepared pan and spread evenly. Cool until set. Cut into squares.

CHOCOLATE HAZELNUT CLUSTERS

makes 2 pounds

9 oz. semi-sweet chocolate, grated or finely chopped
1½ cups hazelnuts

1 tsp. instant espresso powder
1 tsp. canola oil

1. Line a baking sheet with waxed paper.
2. Melt the chocolate. Remove from the heat. Add the hazelnuts, espresso powder, and oil and stir until the nuts are well coated.
3. Drop the mixture by teaspoonfuls onto the prepared baking sheet. Let cool at room temperature until set. Store in an airtight container.

CHOCOLATE NUT CRUNCH

makes 1½ pounds

1¼ cups granulated sugar
1 cup whole almonds
¾ cup butter or margarine
¼ cup water
1½ tsp. salt

½ tsp. baking soda
½ cup chopped walnuts
⅓ cup semi-sweet
    chocolate chips
½ cup ground almonds

1. Grease a 15½ by 10½-inch jelly-roll pan.
2. In a saucepan, over medium heat, combine the sugar, whole almonds, butter, water, and salt. Bring to a boil. Insert a candy thermometer and simmer, stirring frequently, until 290 degrees.
3. Remove from the heat. Stir in the baking soda and walnuts. Immediately pour into the prepared pan. Sprinkle the chocolate chips over the top. Let stand for 3 minutes. Spread the melted chocolate chips over the top. Sprinkle with the ground almonds. Cool in the pan until set. Break into pieces.

CHOCOLATE PEPPERMINT CANDY

makes ¾ to 1 pound

4 oz. semi-sweet chocolate, grated or finely chopped

1½ cups crushed peppermint candies (½ pound, see Baking note)

1. Line a baking sheet with waxed paper.
2. Melt the chocolate. Remove from the heat and stir in the candy.
3. Drop the mixture by teaspoonfuls onto the prepared baking sheet. Chill until firm.

Baking note: Almost any hard candy that can be crushed can be substituted for the peppermint candy. Do not use a food processor to crush the candy, as this will make a powder out of the candy. Place the candy between two sheets of waxed paper and pound it with a food mallet or the bottom of a heavy pan.

CHOCOLATE VANILLA WAFER COOKIE CANDY

makes 1½ to 1¾ pounds

4 oz. semi-sweet chocolate, grated or finely chopped
1 can (14 oz.) sweetened condensed milk
2 cups vanilla wafer cookie crumbs

1 tsp. chocolate or vanilla extract
1 cup pecans, finely chopped
Powdered sugar for coating

1. Lightly grease a 13 by 9-inch pan.
2. In the top of a double boiler over simmering water, melt the chocolate, stirring constantly. Stir in the condensed milk and cook until thickened. Remove from the heat. Stir in the cookie crumbs, chocolate extract, and nuts.
3. Pour the mixture into the prepared pan and spread evenly. Chill for 1 hour, or until set. Cut into squares. Roll each square in powdered sugar. Wrap individually in waxed paper or plastic wrap and chill until serving.

Baking note: For a variation, chocolate wafer cookie crumbs can be used.

EASY CHOCOLATE TRUFFLES

makes 5 dozen truffles

12 oz. semi-sweet chocolate, grated or finely chopped	3 cups powdered sugar
4 oz. cream cheese, at room temperature	1½ tsp. chocolate extract
	Ground almonds for coating

1. Line two baking sheets with waxed paper.
2. Melt the chocolate. Remove from the heat.
3. In a large bowl, using an electric mixer on medium speed, beat the cream cheese until smooth. Beat in the powdered sugar, ½ cup at a time. Beat in the melted chocolate and chocolate extract. Cover and chill for 1 hour or until firm.
4. Pinch off small pieces of the mixture and roll it into 1-inch balls. Roll each truffle in the almonds until well coated. Place on the prepared baking sheets. Chill for 1 to 2 hours or until serving.

Baking note: Chopped pecans, cocoa powder, or toasted coconut can also be used to coat the truffles.

FRENCH CHOCOLATE

makes 50 to 60 candies

1⅓ cups semi-sweet
  chocolate chips
1 cup walnuts, ground

¾ cup sweetened
  condensed milk
1 tsp. crème de cacao
Flaked coconut for coating

1. Line a baking sheet with waxed paper.
2. Melt the chocolate chips. Remove from the heat. Stir in the walnuts, condensed milk, and crème de cacao. Cool for 5 minutes.
3. Pinch off pieces of the mixture and roll into 1-inch balls. Roll each ball in the coconut until well coated. Place the balls on the prepared baking sheet. Chill for 2 hours before serving.

Baking note: Chopped walnuts or powdered sugar can also be used to coat the chocolates.

MARSHMALLOW CHOCOLATE NUT BALLS

makes 24 balls

2 oz. unsweetened chocolate, grated or finely chopped
1⅓ cups sweetened condensed milk

24 large marshmallows
1 cup chopped almonds for coating

1. Line a baking sheet with waxed paper.
2. In the top of a double boiler over simmering water, melt the chocolate, stirring until smooth. Add the condensed milk and cook for 3 to 5 minutes, or until the mixture thickens.
3. Using a bamboo skewer or a fondue fork, dip the marshmallows in the chocolate mixture, coating completely. Roll in the almonds and place on the prepared baking sheet. Cool for 1 hour or until set.

MEXICAN CHOCOLATE TRUFFLES

makes 24 truffles

coating
¼ cup unsweetened
  cocoa powder
1½ tsp. ground cinnamon
truffles
 4 oz. semi-sweet chocolate,
  grated or finely chopped

⅓ cup powdered sugar
⅓ cup almond paste
1 tbsp. strong brewed coffee
1 tsp. butter or margarine,
  melted

1. To make the coating, on a small plate, combine the cocoa powder
   and cinnamon.
2. To make the truffles, mix the chocolate, powdered sugar, almond
   paste, coffee, and butter until it forms a smooth paste. Using a
   tablespoon or melon baller, scoop up the mixture and roll it into
   1-inch balls. Roll each truffle in the coating mixture until well coated.
   Place on a waxed paper-lined baking sheet and chill for 2 hours
   before serving.

Baking note: For a decorative garnish, drizzle melted white or dark
chocolate over the truffles. The truffles can also be made in larger sizes.

MINT CHOCOLATE FUDGE

makes 1½ to 2 pounds

10 oz. semi-sweet chocolate, grated or finely chopped
1 can (14 oz.) sweetened condensed milk
2 tsp. crème de cacao

1 cup white chocolate chips
1 tbsp. peppermint or spearmint schnapps
3 drops green food coloring

1. Line a 9-inch square pan with waxed paper.
2. In a large saucepan, over low heat, melt the semi-sweet chocolate with 1 cup of the condensed milk, stirring until smooth. Remove from the heat and add the crème de cacao. Pour half of the mixture into the prepared pan and spread evenly. Chill for 10 minutes. Keep the remaining chocolate mixture at room temperature.
3. In a medium saucepan, over low heat, melt the white chocolate chips with the remaining condensed milk, stirring until smooth. Remove from the heat and stir in the schnapps and food coloring. Spread this mixture over the top of the chilled chocolate and chill for 10 minutes or until firm.
4. Spread the remaining chocolate mixture on top of the white chocolate mixture and chill for 2 hours or until firm. Invert onto a sheet of waxed paper and peel off the waxed paper from the bottom. Cut into bite-size pieces.

Baking note: Crème de menthe can be used in place of the schnapps.

MOCHA TRUFFLES

makes 1½ to 2 dozen truffles

1¼ cups powdered sugar
3 oz. unsweetened chocolate,
  grated or finely chopped
½ cup butter or margarine,
  melted

2 tbsp. coffee liqueur
4 large egg yolks
½ cup Brazil nuts,
  finely ground for coating

1. In a medium bowl, combine the powdered sugar, grated chocolate, butter, and liqueur. Beat in the egg yolks, one at a time. Chill for 1 hour, or until the mixture is firm enough to form into balls.
2. Using a tablespoon or melon baller, scoop up the mixture and roll into 1-inch balls. Roll each truffle in the nuts until well coated. Place in an airtight container and chill until serving.

Baking note: Due to the raw eggs used in this recipe, keep refrigerated at all times, and for no longer than 1 week.

NOUGAT SQUARES

makes 1½ pounds

3 tbsp. butter or margarine
1 jar (7 oz.) marshmallow creme
4 cups puffed corn cereal
½ cup flaked coconut
¼ cup ground almonds
½ tsp. salt
1 cup semi-sweet chocolate chips

1. Lightly grease a 9-inch square pan.
2. In the top of a double boiler over simmering water, melt the butter with the marshmallow creme, stirring until smooth. Remove from the heat. Add the cereal, coconut, almonds, and salt. Press evenly onto the bottom of the prepared pan.
3. In the top of a double boiler over simmering water, melt the chocolate chips, stirring until smooth. Spread evenly over the top of the mixture in the pan. Chill for 1 hour or until set. Cut into bars.

OPERA
FUDGE

makes 2½ pounds

3 oz. unsweetened chocolate,
grated or finely chopped
1 tbsp. light corn syrup
2 cups granulated sugar
¾ cup heavy cream
½ cup evaporated milk

¾ cup pecans, chopped
1 tsp. chocolate or
vanilla extract
6 oz. semi-sweet chocolate,
grated or finely chopped

1. Lightly grease a 9-inch square pan.
2. In a saucepan over low heat, melt the unsweetened chocolate
   and corn syrup, stirring until smooth. Stir in the sugar, cream, and
   evaporated milk. Insert a candy thermometer and cook, stirring
   occasionally, until 238 degrees. Remove from the heat and stir in the
   pecans and chocolate extract. Pour the mixture into the prepared pan
   and spread evenly. Cool slightly.
3. Melt the semi-sweet chocolate. As soon as the fudge starts to
   harden, spread the melted chocolate over the top. Chill for 1 hour or
   until firm. Cut into bite-size pieces.

PEANUT BUTTER
CHOCOLATE FUDGE

makes 2½ pounds

2 cups peanut butter chips
1 can (14 oz.) sweetened
   condensed milk
¼ cup butter or margarine

½ cup peanuts, chopped
1 cup semi-sweet
   chocolate chips

1. Line an 8-inch square pan with waxed or parchment paper.
2. In a medium saucepan, over low heat, melt the peanut butter chips, 1 cup of the condensed milk, and 2 tablespoon of the butter, stirring constantly until smooth. Remove from the heat and immediately stir in the peanuts. Pour the mixture evenly in the bottom of the prepared pan.
3. In the top of a double boiler over simmering water, melt the chocolate chips, stirring constantly until smooth. Add the remaining condensed milk and butter and stir until blended. Spread evenly over the peanut butter layer in the pan. Chill for 2 hours or until firm. Invert onto a sheet of waxed paper and peel off the waxed paper from the bottom. Cut into squares.

PEANUT MOUND CLUSTERS

makes 1½ pounds

1 cup creamy peanut butter
6 oz. unsweetened chocolate, grated or finely chopped
6 oz. semi-sweet chocolate, grated or finely chopped

½ cup flaked coconut
½ cup raisins
1½ cups salted Spanish peanuts
Flaked coconut for garnish

1. In the top of a double boiler over simmering water, melt the peanut butter and chocolates, stirring until smooth. Remove from the heat and fold in the coconut, raisins, and peanuts.
2. Drop by tablespoonfuls onto a waxed paper-lined baking sheet. Immediately sprinkle coconut over the tops. Let cool until set.

Baking note: The candies can also be spooned into miniature paper candy cups instead of onto a baking sheet.

PECAN CHOCOLATE CLUSTERS

makes 24 to 30 clusters

1 cup pecan halves	2 oz. semi-sweet chocolate,
14 oz. caramel candies	grated or finely chopped
1 tbsp. evaporated milk	1 oz. milk chocolate,
	grated or finely chopped

1. Line a baking sheet with waxed paper.
2. Arrange the pecan halves in clusters on the prepared baking sheet.
3. In a small saucepan, over low heat, melt the caramels with the evaporated milk, stirring until smooth. Remove from the heat and cool for 5 minutes, or until the mixture is thick.
4. Melt the semi-sweet chocolate. Remove from the heat and stir in the milk chocolate, stirring until smooth.
5. Spoon teaspoonfuls of the caramel mixture onto each pecan cluster. Top with a spoonful of the melted chocolate and cool slightly. Cover and chill until firm.

SCOTCH DROPS

makes 1½ pounds

6 oz. semi-sweet chocolate, grated or finely chopped
1 cup butterscotch chips

1 can (7 oz.) salted peanuts, chopped
1 cup puffed rice cereal

1. In the top of a double boiler over simmering water, melt the chocolate and butterscotch chips, stirring until smooth. Stir in the peanuts and the cereal.
2. Drop by teaspoonfuls onto a waxed paper-lined baking sheet. Chill for 1 hour or until solid.

Baking note: The candy can be spooned into miniature paper candy cups instead of onto a baking sheet.

WHITE CHOCOLATE MARSHMALLOW BARS

makes 24 servings

½ cup chopped pecans
1 tbsp. butter or margarine
1⅓ cups miniature
 marshmallows

8 oz. white chocolate or
 almond bark, grated
 or finely chopped

1. Line an 8 by 4-inch loaf pan with waxed paper, allowing the ends of the paper to extend over the two long sides of the pan.
2. In a small skillet, over low heat, sauté the pecans in the butter for 4 to 5 minutes, or until toasted, stirring constantly. Remove from the heat.
3. Arrange half of the marshmallows in a single layer on the bottom of the prepared pan. Do not crowd the marshmallows or let them touch the sides of the pan. Press the chopped pecans into the spaces between the marshmallows.
4. Melt the white chocolate. Pour over the top of the marshmallows in the pan and spread evenly. Gently tap the loaf pan on a flat surface to force the white chocolate to the bottom of the pan. Press the remaining marshmallows evenly into the top of the white chocolate. Chill for 1 hour or until firm.
5. Using the ends of the waxed paper as handles, lift the candy from the pan. Remove the paper and cut into 24 bars.

ALMOND BROWNIE BARS

makes 2 dozen

first layer
½ cup butter or margarine, at room temperature
1 cup ground almonds
⅓ cup granulated sugar
1 cup all-purpose flour

second layer
¼ cup butter or margarine
1 oz. unsweetened chocolate, grated or finely chopped

⅓ cup granulated sugar
1 large egg
¾ cup all-purpose flour

third layer
1 cup almond paste
¼ cup butter or margarine, at room temperature
½ cup granulated sugar
2 large eggs

1. Position a rack in the center of the oven and preheat the oven to 350 degrees. Lightly grease a 9-inch square pan.
2. To make the first layer, in a large bowl, using an electric mixer on medium speed, beat the butter, almonds, sugar, and flour until a crumbly mixture forms. Press evenly onto the bottom of the prepared pan.
3. To make the second layer, in the top of a double boiler over simmering water, melt the butter and chocolate, stirring until smooth. Remove from the heat. Beat in the sugar, egg, and flour until thoroughly blended. Spread evenly over the top of the first layer.
4. To make the third layer, crumble the almond paste into a medium bowl. Using an electric mixer on high speed, beat in the butter, sugar, and eggs. Spread the mixture evenly over the top of the second layer.
5. Bake for 45 to 50 minutes, or until the edges start to pull away from the sides of the pan. The center will be firm. Cool in the pan on a wire rack. Cut into 24 bars.

APRICOT BROWNIES

makes 2 dozen

¼ cup dried apricots, diced
1 tbsp. apricot liqueur
4 oz. semi-sweet chocolate, grated or finely chopped
4 oz. unsweetened chocolate, grated or finely chopped
2 tbsp. butter or margarine
¼ cup all-purpose flour
¼ tsp. baking powder
Pinch of salt
2 large eggs
¾ cup granulated sugar
1 cup pecans or hazelnuts, chopped
1 cup white chocolate chips
¼ cup flaked coconut

1. Position the rack in the center of the oven and preheat the oven to 350 degrees. Lightly grease a 13 by 9-inch pan.
2. Place the apricots in a small bowl and sprinkle with the liqueur. Soak for 10 minutes. Drain and reserve the liqueur.
3. In the top of a double boiler over simmering water, melt the chocolates and butter, stirring until smooth. Remove from the heat.
4. Combine the flour, baking powder, and salt.
5. In a large bowl, using an electric mixer on medium speed, beat the eggs until thick and light-colored. Beat in the sugar and reserved liqueur. Pouring it in a thin stream, beat in the chocolate mixture. Gradually blend in the dry ingredients. Fold in the apricots, pecans, white chocolate chips, and coconut. Pour the mixture into the prepared pan and spread evenly.
6. Bake for 12 to 15 minutes, or until a cake tester inserted into the center comes out clean. Cool in the pan on a wire rack. Cut into 24 bars.

BASIC BROWNIE
MASTER MIX

makes 14 cups brownie mix

3 cups all-purpose flour
2 cups unsweetened cocoa
  powder
1 tbsp. baking powder

2 tsp. salt
3½ cups vegetable shortening
  (see Baking note)
5 cups granulated sugar

1. To make the brownie master mix: combine the flour, cocoa powder, baking powder, and salt.
2. In a large bowl, using an electric mixer on medium speed, beat the vegetable shortening and sugar until smooth. Gradually blend in the dry ingredients. Store in an airtight container at room temperature until ready to use. This lasts for up to 1 year.
3. To make the brownies, position a rack in the center of the oven and preheat the oven to 350 degrees. Grease a 9-inch square pan.
4. Place 2¾ cups of the Basic Brownie Master Mix in a large bowl. Add 2 beaten large eggs and 1 tsp. vanilla extract. Using an electric mixer on medium speed, beat until thoroughly mixed.
5. Pour the mixture into the prepared pan and spread evenly.
6. Bake for 25 to 30 minutes, or until a cake tester inserted into the center comes out clean. Cool in the pan on a wire rack. Cut into 12 bars.

Baking note: Use vegetable shortening that does not require refrigeration. This mix will make 5 single recipes.

BISCOTTI
WITH MASCARPONE
makes 8 servings

3 large eggs, separated
Pinch of salt
⅔ cup powdered sugar
10 oz. mascarpone cheese
  (1¼ cups)

¼ cup dark rum
1 package (7 oz.) biscotti
⅓ cup strong brewed coffee
2 tbsp. semi-sweet chocolate,
  grated

1. In a medium bowl, using an electric mixer on medium speed,
   beat the egg whites and salt until stiff but not dry.
2. In a large bowl, using an electric mixer on medium speed, beat the
   egg yolks and powdered sugar until thick and light-colored. Add the
   mascarpone and rum and beat until smooth. Fold in the egg whites.
3. Arrange the biscotti on a shallow serving plate and sprinkle the
   coffee over the top. Spread the mascarpone mixture evenly over the
   biscotti. Sprinkle the chocolate over the top. Chill for 8 to 10 hours,
   or until serving.

Baking note: Due to the raw eggs used in this recipe, it should be kept
refrigerated at all times, and for no longer than 3 to 5 days.

BROWNIES WITH RAISINS AND MARSHMALLOWS

makes 12 servings

½ cup all-purpose flour
½ tsp. salt
¼ cup vegetable shortening
2 oz. semi-sweet chocolate,
  grated or finely chopped
1 cup granulated sugar

1 tsp. vanilla or
  chocolate extract
2 large eggs
1 cup raisins
1 cup miniature marshmallows

1. Position a rack in the center of the oven and preheat the oven to 325 degrees. Lightly grease an 8-inch square pan.
2. Combine the flour and salt.
3. In a double boiler over simmering water, melt the shortening and chocolate, stirring until smooth. Remove from the heat. Using an electric mixer on medium speed, beat in the sugar and vanilla extract. On high speed, beat in the eggs. Gradually blend in the dry ingredients. Fold in the raisins and marshmallows. Pour the mixture into the prepared pan and spread evenly.
4. Bake for 20 to 25 minutes, or until a cake tester inserted into the center comes out clean. Cool in the pan on a wire rack. Cut into 12 squares.

BUTTERMILK
BROWNIES

makes 3 dozen

brownies
2 cups all-purpose flour
1 tsp. baking soda
½ tsp. salt
1 cup butter or margarine
1 cup water
⅓ cup Dutch processed cocoa
   powder
2 cups granulated sugar

½ cup buttermilk
2 large eggs
1 tsp. crème de cacao
frosting
½ cup butter or margarine
6 tbsp. buttermilk
⅓ cup Dutch processed
   cocoa powder
½ cup powdered sugar

1. Position a rack in the center of the oven and preheat the oven to
   350 degrees. Grease a 15½ by 10½-inch jelly-roll pan.
2. To make the brownies, in a large bowl, combine the flour, baking
   soda, and salt.
3. In a large saucepan, over medium heat, melt the butter. Add the
   water and cocoa powder, stirring until smooth. Remove from the heat
   and stir in the sugar until dissolved. Add the dry ingredients and mix
   until combined. Beat in the buttermilk, eggs, and crème de cacao.
   Pour the mixture into the prepared pan and spread evenly.
4. Bake for 15 to 18 minutes, or until a cake tester inserted into the
   center comes out clean. Cool in the pan on a wire rack.
5. To make the frosting, in a medium saucepan, over medium heat, melt
   the butter. Mix in the buttermilk and cocoa powder. Bring to a boil
   and simmer for 1 minute.
6. Beat in the powdered sugar until just mixed. Cool for 5 minutes
   at room temperature and spread over the brownies.

CHOCOLATE ALMOND COOKIES
makes 2 dozen

crust
1 envelope premelted
   unsweetened chocolate
¼ cup butter or margarine
1 large egg
½ cup granulated sugar
¼ cup all-purpose flour
¼ cup sliced almonds

filling
1 cup powdered sugar
2 tbsp. butter or margarine,
   at room temperature
1 tbsp. evaporated milk
¼ tsp. almond extract
topping
1 oz. semi-sweet chocolate
1 tbsp. butter or margarine

1. Position a rack in the center of the oven and preheat the oven to
   350 degrees. Lightly grease an 8-inch square pan.
2. To make the crust, in the top of a double boiler over simmering water, melt
   the chocolate and butter, stirring until smooth. Remove from the heat.
3. In a medium bowl, using an electric mixer on medium speed, beat the
   egg until thick and light-colored. Beat in the chocolate mixture and
   sugar. Gradually blend in the flour. Fold in the almonds and mix
   thoroughly. Pour the mixture into the prepared pan and spread evenly.
4. Bake for 15 to 20 minutes, or until a cake tester inserted into the
   center comes out clean. Cool in the pan for 20 minutes.
5. To make the filling, in a small bowl, blend the powdered sugar,
   butter, evaporated milk, and almond extract. Spread evenly over the
   baked crust and chill for 30 minutes.
6. To make the topping, in the top of a double boiler over simmering
   water, melt the chocolate and butter, stirring until smooth. Drizzle
   over the top of the filling and chill for 20 minutes. Cut into 24 bars.

CHOCOLATE BROWNIES

makes 1 dozen

¾ cup all-purpose flour
½ tsp. baking powder
½ tsp. salt
2 oz. unsweetened chocolate, grated or finely chopped
⅓ cup butter or margarine

1 cup granulated sugar
1 tsp. vanilla
   or chocolate extract
2 large eggs
½ cup walnuts or pecans, chopped

1. Position a rack in the center of the oven and preheat the oven to 350 degrees. Lightly grease a 9-inch square pan.
2. Combine the flour, baking powder, and salt.
3. In the top of a double boiler over simmering water, melt the chocolate and butter, stirring until smooth. Remove from the heat.
4. Transfer the melted chocolate and butter into a large bowl. Using an electric mixer, beat in the sugar and flavored extract. Beat in the eggs. Gradually blend in the dry ingredients. Fold in the walnuts. Pour the mixture into the prepared pan and spread evenly.
5. Bake for 30 to 35 minutes, or until a cake tester inserted into the center comes out clean. Cool in the pan on a wire rack. Cut into 12 bars.

CHOCOLATE
BUTTER BALLS

makes 2 to 3 dozen

1 cup ground almonds
⅔ cup all-purpose flour
¼ cup Dutch processed
cocoa powder

½ cup butter or margarine,
at room temperature
3 tbsp. powdered sugar
Powdered sugar for rolling

1. Position a rack in the center of the oven and preheat the oven to
   350 degrees.
2. Combine the almonds, flour and cocoa powder.
3. In a medium bowl, using an electric mixer on medium speed,
   beat the butter and the 3 tablespoons of powdered sugar. Gradually
   blend in the dry ingredients. The dough will be stiff. Pinch off pieces
   of the dough, roll into balls, and place 1 inch apart on an ungreased
   baking sheet.
4. Bake for 15 to 20 minutes, or until light golden brown. Roll the hot
   cookies in powdered sugar and transfer to a wire rack to cool.
   When completely cool, roll in the powdered sugar again.

CHOCOLATE
CARAMEL BARS

makes 2 dozen

crust
2 cups all-purpose flour
1 cup packed light-brown
  sugar
½ cup butter or margarine
1 cup pecans or almonds,
  finely ground

filling
1 cup butter or margarine
¾ cup packed light-brown sugar
topping
2 cups semi-sweet or
  white chocolate chips

1. Position a rack in the center of the oven and preheat the oven to
   350 degrees. Lightly grease a 13 by 9-inch pan.
2. To make the crust, in a large bowl, combine the flour and brown
   sugar. Using a pastry blender, cut in the butter, until the mixture
   forms coarse crumbs. Press onto the bottom of the prepared pan.
   Sprinkle the pecans evenly over the top.
3. To make the filling, in a saucepan, over medium heat, combine the
   butter and brown sugar. Stirring constantly, bring to a boil and cook
   for 1 minute. Spread evenly over the crust in the pan.
4. Bake for 15 to 20 minutes, or until the surface is bubbly. Sprinkle the
   chocolate chips over the top. Let stand for 3 minutes. Spread the melted
   chocolate chips evenly over the top. Cool in the pan on a wire rack.
   Cut into 24 bars.

CHOCOLATE CHARLIES

makes 12 to 14 dozen

3¼ cups all-purpose flour
¼ cup Dutch processed cocoa powder
1 tsp. baking soda
¼ tsp. ground cinnamon
½ tsp. salt
1 cup vegetable shortening
1½ cups packed light-brown sugar
2 large eggs
1 cup crème de cacao
Semi-sweet chocolate chips for garnish

1. Position a rack in the center of the oven and preheat the oven to 350 degrees. Lightly grease two baking sheets.
2. Combine the flour, cocoa powder, baking soda, cinnamon, and salt.
3. In a large bowl, using an electric mixer on medium speed, beat the shortening and brown sugar until fluffy. Beat in the eggs. Gradually blend in the dry ingredients, alternating with the crème de cacao. Cover and chill for at least 2 hours.
4. Fill a pastry bag fitted with a large star tip with the dough. Pipe out stars onto the prepared baking sheets, spacing them 1 inch apart. Place a single chocolate chip into the center of each star.
5. Bake for 10 to 12 minutes, or until a golden brown. Transfer to wire racks to cool.

Baking note: Chilling the dough keeps the cookies from spreading out while baking. White chocolate chips can be used in place of the semi-sweet chocolate chips. The dough can also be dropped by teaspoonfuls instead of using a pastry bag.

CHOCOLATE CHEWS

makes 2 dozen

½ cup vegetable shortening
2 oz. unsweetened chocolate,
  grated or finely chopped
2 large eggs
1 cup granulated sugar

½ tsp. almond or
  hazelnut extract
½ cup all-purpose flour
1 cup slivered almonds

1. Position a rack in the center of the oven and preheat the oven
   to 350 degrees. Lightly grease a 13 by 9-inch pan.
2. In the top of a double boiler over simmering water, melt the
   shortening and chocolate, stirring until smooth. Remove from the heat.
3. Transfer the melted chocolate and shortening into a large bowl.
   Using an electric mixer on medium speed, beat in the eggs, one at a
   time, beating well after each addition. Beat in the sugar and almond
   extract. Blend in the flour. Pour the mixture into the prepared pan
   and spread evenly. Sprinkle the slivered almonds over the top.
4. Bake for 35 to 40 minutes, or until a cake tester inserted into the center
   comes out clean. Cool in the pan on a wire rack. Cut into 24 bars.

CHOCOLATE CHIP
MANDELS

makes 3 to 4 dozen

3 cups all-purpose flour
3 tbsp. Dutch processed
    cocoa powder
2 tsp. baking powder
¼ tsp. salt

3 large eggs
1 cup canola oil
1 cup granulated sugar
2 cups semi-sweet
    chocolate chips

1. Position a rack in the center of the oven and preheat the oven to
   350 degrees. Lightly grease a baking sheet.
2. Combine the flour, cocoa powder, baking powder, and salt.
3. In a large bowl, using an electric mixer on medium, beat the eggs
   until thick and light-colored. Beat in the canola oil. Beat in the sugar.
   Gradually stir in the dry ingredients. Fold in the chocolate chips.
4. Divide the dough in half and form each half into a log 3 inches in
   diameter. Place the logs 1½ inches apart on the prepared baking
   sheet.
5. Bake for 30 minutes, or until a cake tester inserted into the center
   comes out clean. Cool on the baking sheet for 10 minutes. Cut each
   log in half lengthwise and cut each half into 1-inch slices. Transfer to
   wire racks to cool completely.

CHOCOLATE CHIP PEANUT LOGS

makes 2 dozen

1 cup semi-sweet chocolate chips	**½ cup peanuts, chopped (optional)**
½ cup creamy peanut butter	**4 cups puffed rice cereal**

1. Lightly grease a 9-inch square pan.
2. In the top of a double boiler over simmering water, melt the chocolate chips and peanut butter. Remove from the heat. Blend in the chopped peanuts. Gradually blend in the cereal. Be sure the cereal is well coated with the chocolate mixture.
3. Pour the mixture into the prepared pan and spread evenly. Cool in the pan on a wire rack until the mixture hardens slightly. Chill for 30 minutes in the refrigerator.
4. Cut into 24 bars. Roll the bars between your palms to form logs. Wrap individually in waxed paper or plastic wrap and store tightly covered until serving.

Baking note: This is a great recipe to make with children. Let them roll the logs.

CHOCOLATE
CHRISTMAS COOKIES

makes 2 to 3 dozen

1 cup all-purpose flour
1 cup whole wheat flour
½ cup soy flour
1 cup Dutch processed
 cocoa powder
½ tsp. baking soda
1 tsp. ground allspice
Pinch of salt

1 cup butter or margarine,
 at room temperature
2 cups granulated sugar
1 tsp. chocolate or
 vanilla extract
1 large egg
1 tbsp. crème de cacao
Sweetened cocoa powder
 for garnish

1. Position a rack in the center of the oven and preheat the oven
   to 400 degrees. Lightly grease two baking sheets.
2. Combine the flours, cocoa powder, baking soda, allspice, and salt.
3. In a large bowl, using an electric mixer on medium speed, beat the
   butter, sugar, and flavored extract until light and fluffy. Beat in the
   egg and crème de cacao. Gradually stir in the dry ingredients.
4. On a floured surface, knead the dough until smooth. Roll out the
   dough to a thickness of ⅛ to ¼ inch. Using a 2-inch round cookie
   cutter or floured glass, cut the dough into rounds. Place 1 inch apart
   on the prepared baking sheets. Sprinkle the tops with sweetened
   cocoa powder.
5. Bake for 8 to 10 minutes, or until the cookies look very dry.
   Do not overbake. Transfer to wire racks to cool.

Baking note: This recipe can be used to make sandwich cookies:
fill the cookies with any prepared icing.

CHOCOLATE-COATED MACAROONS

makes 2 to 3 dozen

4 large egg whites
1⅓ cups granulated sugar
1½ tsp. almond extract
¼ tsp. salt
2½ cups flaked coconut

6 tbsp. all-purpose flour
4 oz. unsweetened chocolate, grated or finely chopped
4 oz. semi-sweet chocolate, grated or finely chopped

1. Position a rack in the center of the oven and preheat to 300 degrees.
2. To make the macaroons, in a saucepan, combine the egg whites, sugar, almond extract, and salt and stir until thoroughly blended. Blend in the coconut and flour. Place over medium heat and cook, stirring constantly, for 5 minutes. Raise the heat to medium-high and cook, stirring constantly, for 4 minutes, or until the mixture is thick and pulls away from the sides of the pan. Immediately transfer to a large bowl and cool for 5 minutes. Cover and chill for at least 10 minutes, or until the dough is cold.
3. Drop the dough by teaspoonfuls 1½ inches apart onto two lightly greased baking sheets.
4. Bake for 20 to 25 minutes, or until a light golden brown. Transfer to wire racks to cool completely.
5. To make the coating, in the top of a double boiler over simmering water, melt the chocolates, stirring constantly until smooth. Remove from the heat.
6. Line a baking sheet with waxed paper. Dip the macaroons into the chocolate, coating half of each cookie, and chill on the prepared baking sheet until the chocolate has hardened. Coat the other half with chocolate and let harden.

CHOCOLATE COCONUT TOFFEE BARS

makes 8 to 10 servings

1¼ cups all-purpose flour
⅓ cup Dutch processed cocoa powder
¾ cup butter-flavored vegetable shortening
1 cup powdered sugar
2 tbsp. butter or margarine

1 can (14 oz.) sweetened condensed milk
2 tsp. chocolate or almond extract
1 cup semi-sweet chocolate chips
½ cup flaked coconut

1. Position a rack in the center of the oven and preheat the oven to 350 degrees. Lightly grease a 13 by 9-inch pan.
2. Combine the flour and cocoa powder.
3. In a large bowl, using an electric mixer on medium speed, beat the shortening and sugar until fluffy. Gradually blend in the dry ingredients. Pour mixture into the prepared pan and spread evenly.
4. Bake for 15 minutes.
5. In the top of a double boiler over simmering water, melt the butter with the milk until thickened. (It will take about 15 minutes.) Remove from the heat and stir in the flavored extract. Immediately pour this over the baked crust.
6. Bake for 10 minutes, or until a cake tester inserted into the center comes out clean.
7. Sprinkle the chocolate chips evenly over the top and bake for 3 to 5 minutes, or until the chocolate is melted. Remove from the oven. Using a knife, spread the melted chocolate chips over the top. Sprinkle with the coconut. Cool in the pan on a wire rack. Cut into bars.

CHOCOLATE COOKIE KISSES

makes 2 to 3 dozen

2 oz. unsweetened chocolate, **¼ tsp. cream of tartar**
  grated or finely chopped **1 cup granulated sugar**
4 large egg whites **¼ tsp. almond extract**
¼ tsp. salt

1. Position a rack in the center of the oven and preheat the oven to 250 degrees. Line two baking sheets with wax or parchment paper.
2. Melt the chocolate. Remove from the heat.
3. In a large bowl, using an electric mixer on high speed, beat the egg whites until foamy. Beat in the sugar. Mix in the salt and cream of tartar. Add the almond extract and beat until the mixture forms stiff peaks. Fold in the melted chocolate. Drop the mixture by spoonfuls 1 inch apart onto the prepared baking sheets.
4. Bake for 35 to 40 minutes, or until firm to the touch. Transfer to wire racks to cool.

Baking note: For crisper kisses, turn the oven off after baking and leave the baking sheet in the oven until the cookies are cool. (Do not open the oven door.)

CHOCOLATE CORNUCOPIAS

makes 11/2 to 2 dozen

1 cup semi-sweet
  chocolate chips
½ cup vegetable shortening
½ cup granulated sugar
Pinch of salt
¼ tsp. ground ginger
⅓ cup light corn syrup
1 cup plus 2 tbsp.
  all-purpose flour

8 oz. cream cheese,
  at room temperature
2 cups heavy cream
½ tsp. chocolate or
  vanilla extract
2 oz. semi-sweet chocolate,
  grated or finely chopped

1. Position a rack in the center of the oven and preheat the oven to
   350 degrees. Grease two baking sheets.
2. To make the cookies, in the top of a double boiler over simmering
   water, melt the chocolate chips, stirring until smooth. Stir in
   shortening, sugar, salt, and ginger until smooth. Remove from the
   heat. Using a wooden spoon, blend in the corn syrup and flour. Drop
   by tablespoonfuls 3 inches apart onto the prepared baking sheets.
3. To make the filling, using an electric mixer on medium speed, beat
   the cream cheese until very soft. Add the cream and flavored extract.
   Whip on high speed until soft peaks form. Fold in the grated chocolate.
4. Bake for 8 to 10 minutes, or until dry-looking. Cool on the baking
   sheet for 1 to 2 minutes. Remove the cookies and shape into
   cornucopia cone by using a cone mold or roll into cones. Lay on a
   wire rack to cool completely, seam-side down.
5. When the cookies are cool, fill a pastry bag with a medium star tip.
   Pipe the filling into the cookies.

CHOCOLATE CREAM DREAM BARS

makes 3 dozen

crust

2½ cups all-purpose flour

2 cups old-fashioned oats

1½ cups packed light-brown sugar

1 tsp. baking soda

¼ tsp. salt

1 cup butter-flavored vegetable shortening or margarine

filling

2 cups semi-sweet chocolate chips

1 can (14 oz.) sweetened condensed milk

2 tbsp. butter-flavored vegetable shortening or margarine

2 tsp. chocolate or vanilla extract

1 cup pecans, finely chopped (optional)

1. Position a rack in the center of the oven and preheat the oven to 350 degrees.
2. To make the crust, in a large bowl, combine the flour, oats, brown sugar, baking soda, and salt. Using a pastry blender, cut in the shortening to make a crumbly mixture. Press 4 cups onto the bottom of an ungreased 15½ by 10½-inch jelly-roll pan. Reserve the remaining crust mixture.
3. To make the filling, in the top of a double boiler over simmering water, melt the chocolate chips, stirring until smooth. Add the condensed milk and shortening and heat thoroughly. Remove from the heat and stir in the flavored extract and pecans. Immediately pour over the crust in the pan. Sprinkle with the reserved crust mixture.
4. Bake for 25 to 30 minutes, or until a cake tester inserted into the center comes out clean. Cool in the pan on a wire rack. Cut into 36 bars.

CHOCOLATE CRINKLES

makes 3 to 4 dozen

2 cups all-purpose flour
2 tsp. baking powder
3 oz. semi-sweet chocolate,
  grated or finely chopped
½ cup canola oil
1½ cups granulated sugar

1 tsp. vanilla or
  chocolate extract
2 large eggs
¼ cup milk
Powdered sugar for rolling

1. Position a rack in the center of the oven and preheat the oven
   to 350 degrees. Lightly grease two baking sheets.
2. Combine the flour and baking powder.
3. Melt the chocolate. Remove from the heat.
4. In a large bowl, using an electric mixer on medium speed, beat the
   oil, sugar, and flavored extract until smooth. Beat in the eggs, one at
   a time, beating well after each addition. Beat in the melted
   chocolate. Beat in the milk. Gradually stir in the dry ingredients.
5. Pinch off walnut-sized pieces of the dough and roll into balls.
   Roll each ball in powdered sugar and place 1½ inches apart on the
   prepared baking pans.
6. Bake for 12 to 15 minutes, or until firm to the touch. Roll in
   powdered sugar again while still warm. Transfer to wire racks to cool.

CHOCOLATE DELIGHT BARS

makes 1 dozen

½ cup butter or margarine, at room temperature

3 tbsp. powdered sugar

2 large eggs yolks (reserve the whites for topping)

1 tsp. instant coffee powder

1 tbsp. warm water

2 cups all-purpose flour

½ cup semi-sweet chocolate chips

2 large egg whites

¼ granulated sugar

¼ cup almonds, finely ground

¼ cup almonds, chopped, for garnish

1. Position a rack in the center of the oven and preheat the oven to 350 degrees. Lightly grease a 9-inch square pan.

2. In a large bowl, using an electric mixer on medium speed, beat the butter, powdered sugar, egg yolks, coffee powder, and water until smooth. Gradually blend in the flour. The mixture will be crumbly. Pour the mixture into the prepared pan and spread evenly.

3. Bake for 20 minutes. Remove from the oven. While the crust is baking, make the topping.

4. To make the topping, melt the chocolate. Remove from the heat.

5. In a medium bowl, using an electric mixer on high speed, beat the egg whites until foamy. Beat in the granulated sugar and beat until stiff peaks form. Pouring it in a steady stream, beat in the melted chocolate. Fold in the ground almonds.

6. Spread the topping mixture over the hot crust, sprinkle with the chopped almonds, and bake for 20 minutes longer, or until a cake tester inserted into the center comes out clean. Cool in the pan on a wire rack. Cut into 12 bars.

CHOCOLATE-DIPPED
HEALTH FOOD COOKIES

makes 2 dozen

3 cups granola
½ cup raisins
½ cup chopped unsalted
  peanuts
½ cup flaked coconut
¾ cup chunky peanut butter

½ cup light corn syrup
½ cup honey
2 lbs. semi-sweet chocolate,
  grated

1. Lightly grease a 13 by 9-inch baking pan.
2. In a large bowl, combine the granola, raisins, peanuts, and coconut.
3. In a saucepan, over medium heat, combine the peanut butter, corn
   syrup, and honey. Bring to a boil and cook for 1 minute. Remove
   from the heat. Add to the dry ingredients. Using a wooden spoon,
   stir until everything is well coated. Pour the mixture into the prepared
   pan and spread evenly. Chill for 30 minutes. Cut into 24 bars.
4. Melt the chocolate in a double boiler over hot water, stirring
   constantly. Remove from heat.
5. Dip the bars into the chocolate, coating half of each bar. Place on a
   sheet of waxed paper to set. When the chocolate has hardened, dip
   the other half in the chocolate and place on the waxed paper to set.
   Individually wrap the bars in waxed paper or plastic wrap and chill
   until serving.

CHOCOLATE FUDGE
CHEESECAKE BARS

makes 2 dozen

4 oz. unsweetened chocolate, grated or finely chopped
1 cup butter or margarine
4 large eggs
2 cups granulated sugar

1 tsp. almond or chocolate extract
8 oz. cream cheese, at room temperature
2 cups all-purpose flour

1. Position a rack in the center of the oven and preheat the oven to 350 degrees. Lightly grease a 13 by 9-inch pan.
2. In the top of a double boiler over simmering water, melt the chocolate and butter, stirring until smooth. Remove from the heat.
3. In a medium bowl, using an electric mixer on medium speed, beat the eggs until thick and light-colored. Beat in the sugar and flavored extract just until blended. On low speed, beat in the chocolate mixture, pouring it in a thin stream. Blend in the cream cheese. Gradually blend in the flour. Pour the mixture into the prepared pan and spread evenly.
4. Bake for 20 to 25 minutes, or until dough pulls away from the sides of the pan. Cool in the pan on a wire rack. Chill for about 30 minutes. Cut into 24 bars.

CRÈME DE MENTHE BARS
makes 12 to 16 bars

bottom layer
½ cup butter or margarine
½ cup Dutch processed
  cocoa powder
½ cup powdered sugar
1 large egg, beaten
1 tsp. white crème de menthe
2 cups graham cracker crumbs

middle layer
½ cup butter or margarine
⅓ cup green crème de menthe
3 cups powdered sugar
top layer
¼ cup butter or margarine
1½ cups semi-sweet
  chocolate chips

1. To make the bottom layer, in a medium saucepan, over low heat, melt the butter. Add the cocoa powder, stirring until smooth. Remove from the heat and add the powdered sugar, egg, and white crème de menthe. Stir in the graham cracker crumbs. Pour the mixture into the bottom of an ungreased 13 by 9-inch pan and spread evenly.
2. To make the middle layer, in a medium saucepan, over low heat, melt the butter. Remove from the heat and stir in the green crème de menthe. Gradually blend in the powdered sugar. Spread evenly over the bottom layer in the pan.
3. To make the top layer, in the top of a double boiler over simmering water, melt the butter and chocolate chips, stirring until smooth. Spread this mixture evenly over the middle layer. Chill for 30 minutes, or until firm. Cut into 12 to 16 bars.

Baking notes: Due to the raw egg used in this recipe, it should be kept refrigerated at all times, and for no longer than 3 days.

CHOCOLATE MINT BARS
WITH ALMONDS

makes 2 dozen

2 cups all-purpose flour
½ tsp. baking powder
½ cup slivered almonds
1 cup mint chocolate chips
8 oz. cream cheese,
    at room temperature
¾ cup butter or margarine,
    at room temperature

¾ cup granulated sugar
1 tsp. vanilla or
    chocolate extract
1 cup semi-sweet chocolate
    chips for garnish
½ cup chopped almonds
    for garnish

1. Position a rack in the center of the oven and preheat the oven
   to 375 degrees. Grease a 13 by 9-inch pan.
2. Combine the flour, baking powder, almonds, and mint chocolate chips.
3. In a large bowl, using an electric mixer on medium speed, beat the
   cream cheese, butter, and sugar until blended. Beat in the flavored
   extract. Gradually stir in the dry ingredients. Pour the mixture into
   the prepared pan and spread evenly.
4. Bake for 12 to 15 minutes, or until a cake tester inserted into the
   center comes out clean. Sprinkle the chocolate chips over the top.
   Let stand for 3 minutes. Spread the melted chocolate chips evenly
   over the top. Sprinkle with the chopped almonds and cool completely
   on a wire rack. Cut into 24 bars.

CHOCOLATE
SANDWICH COOKIES

makes 2 to 3 dozen

2 cups all-purpose flour
¼ tsp. baking soda
¼ tsp. allspice
¼ tsp. salt
½ cup butter or margarine,
  at room temperature
⅔ cup packed light-brown
  sugar

1 large egg
½ tsp. chocolate
  or vanilla extract
1 cup semi-sweet chocolate
  chips for filling

1. Combine the flour, baking soda, allspice, and salt.
2. In a large bowl, using an electric mixer on medium speed, beat the
   butter and brown sugar until smooth. Beat in the egg and flavored
   extract. Gradually stir in the dry ingredients. The dough will be stiff.
   Form the dough into a log 3 inches in diameter. Wrap with waxed
   paper and chill overnight.
3. Position a rack in the center of the oven and preheat the oven to
   350 degrees.
4. Cut the chilled log into ⅛-inch slices. Place the slices ¾ inch apart on
   an ungreased baking sheet.
5. Bake for 10 to 12 minutes, or until lightly colored. Transfer to wire
   rack to cool.
6. Melt the chocolate chips. Place the cookies bottom-side up, and spread
   a thin layer of the melted chocolate on half of the cookies. Top with
   the remaining cookies bottom side down, to form sandwich cookies.

CHOCOLATE
ICE CREAM CAKE

makes 8 to 10 servings

3 cups chocolate wafer
cookie crumbs
½ cup chopped pecans
1 cup semi-sweet
chocolate chips
½ cup butter or margarine,
melted

1 pint chocolate ice cream,
softened
1 pint vanilla ice cream,
softened
1 pint heavy cream
Ground pecans for garnish

1. In a large bowl, blend the cookie crumbs, pecans, chocolate chips,
   and melted butter. Pour one-third of this mixture into the bottom of
   a 9-inch springform pan and spread evenly.
2. Spread the chocolate ice cream over the crumb mixture and top
   with half of the remaining crumb mixture. Spread with the vanilla
   ice cream and top with the remaining crumbs. Cover and freeze
   for 4 hours.
3. In a medium bowl, using an electric mixture on high, whip the cream
   until soft peaks form.
4. To assemble, remove the side of the pan and transfer the cake to a
   serving plate. Frost the top and sides with whipped cream and sprinkle
   with the pecans.

Baking note: For a variation, use lime or raspberry sherbet in place of the
vanilla ice cream.

CHOCOLATE
ICE CREAM PIE
makes 8 to 10 servings

meringue crust
¾ cup granulated sugar
2 tbsp. Dutch processed
cocoa powder
3 large egg whites
¼ tsp. cream of tartar
Pinch of salt

chocolate filling
1 package (3.4 oz.) chocolate
instant pudding mix
¼ cup milk
1 pint chocolate ice cream,
softened
½ cup heavy cream
Sliced fresh fruit for garnish

1. Position a rack in the center of the oven and preheat the oven
   to 275 degrees. Lightly grease a 9-inch pie pan.
2. To make the crust, combine the sugar and cocoa powder.
3. In a medium bowl, using an electric mixer on high speed, beat the
   egg whites, cream of tartar, and salt until foamy. Sprinkle the sugar
   and cocoa powder over the top and beat until stiff but not dry. Pour
   the mixture evenly over the bottom and sides of the prepared pan.
4. Bake for 1 hour. Cool in the pan on a wire rack.
5. To make the filling, in a medium bowl, using an electric mixer on
   medium speed, beat the pudding mix and milk. Add the softened ice
   cream and beat for 2 minutes. Pour the mixture into the cooled shell
   and freeze for at least 8 hours.
6. In a small bowl, using an electric mixer on high speed, whip the
   cream until stiff peaks form. Spread over the top of the pie and
   freeze for 1 hour. When ready to serve, arrange the sliced fruit over
   the top of the whipped cream.

CHOCOLATE
MARSHMALLOW FREEZE
makes 1 pint

1 can (14 oz.) evaporated milk
⅓ cup Dutch processed
cocoa powder

¼ cup granulated sugar
¼ cup marshmallow creme
Chocolate sauce for serving

1. Measure and reserve ½ cup of the evaporated milk. Place the remaining evaporated milk in a medium bowl and place in the freezer until ready to whip.
2. In a medium saucepan, over low heat, combine the cocoa powder and sugar, stirring until smooth and the sugar is dissolved. Stir in the reserved evaporated milk. Add the marshmallow creme and cook until blended. Remove from the heat and set the pan in a large bowl of ice and water. Stir until completely cool.
3. Using an electric mixer on high speed, beat the chilled evaporated milk until stiff peaks form. Fold in the cocoa mixture and pour into a 9-inch square pan. Cover and freeze for 1 hour, or until firm. Serve with chocolate sauce on the side.

CHOCOLATE MINT
ICE CREAM PIE

makes 8 to 10 servings

1 prepared chocolate
   cookie crumb crust
1 quart chocolate mint ice
   cream, softened
1 cup miniature
   chocolate chips

2 cups chocolate fudge sauce
1 cup chocolate syrup
   for garnish
1 cup heavy cream

1. Bake the prepared pie crust.
2. Spread half of the ice cream over the baked and cooled pie crust.
   Sprinkle the chocolate chips on the top. Spread the remaining ice
   cream over the top. Cover and freeze 1 hour, or until firm.
3. In a medium bowl, using an electric mixer on high speed, whip the
   cream until soft peaks form.
4. To serve, spread the fudge sauce over the pie. Spread the whipped
   cream over the sauce. Drizzle with the chocolate syrup.

CHOCOLATE MOUSSE PIE

makes 8 to 10 servings

1 prepared chocolate
  pastry crust
1½ tsp. unflavored gelatin
1 tbsp. cold water
2 tbsp. boiling water
½ cup plus 1 tbsp.
  granulated sugar

1¼ cups heavy cream
⅓ cup Dutch processed
  cocoa powder
1 tsp. chocolate extract

1. Bake the prepared pie crust.
2. To make the filling, in a cup, sprinkle the gelatin over the cold water.
   Let stand for 2 minutes to soften. Add the boiling water and stir until
   the gelatin is completely dissolved.
3. In the top of a double boiler over simmering water, combine ½ cup
   of the sugar, ½ cup of the cream, the cocoa powder, and the
   chocolate extract. Using an electric mixer on medium speed, beat
   until the mixture thickens. Remove from the heat and beat in the
   gelatin mixture. Pour the mixture into the prepared pastry crust and
   chill for 2 hours.
4. To serve, in a large bowl, using an electric mixer on high speed, whip
   the remaining ¾ cup cream and 1 tablespoon sugar until soft peaks
   form. Spread over the top of the pie.

CHOCOLATE PECAN PIE

makes 8 to 10 servings

pie
1 prepared pastry shell
1½ cups pecans, chopped
1 cup unsweetened chocolate chips
2 large eggs
½ cup light corn syrup
½ cup granulated sugar

¼ cup butter or margarine, melted
chocolate whipped cream
3 tbsp. powdered sugar
2 tbsp. Dutch processed cocoa powder
1 cup heavy cream
½ tsp. crème de cacao

1. Lightly brown the pie crust as directed.
2. Sprinkle the pecans and chocolate chips over the bottom of the prepared crust.
3. In a medium bowl, using an electric mixer on medium speed, beat the eggs, corn syrup, and sugar until smooth. Beat in the melted butter until blended. Pour the mixture into the prepared crust and spread evenly.
4. Bake for 60 minutes, or until a cake tester inserted into the center comes out clean. Cool on a wire rack for 10 minutes.
5. In a cup, combine the powdered sugar and cocoa powder. In a medium bowl, using an electric mixer on high speed, whip the cream until soft peaks form. Fold in the dry ingredients. Fold in the crème de cacao. Chill for 30 minutes. Spread over the top of the pie before serving.

FUDGE PECAN PIE

makes 8 to 10 servings

1 prepared chocolate
pastry crust
4 oz. semi-sweet chocolate,
grated or finely chopped
¼ cup butter-flavored
vegetable shortening
1 can (14 oz.) sweetened
condensed milk

2 large eggs
¼ cup hot water
1 tsp. almond extract
Pinch of salt
½ cup pecan pieces
½ cup granulated sugar
2 tbsp. chocolate liqueur

1. Position a rack in the center of the oven and preheat the oven
   to 400 degrees.
2. Make and bake the pie crust. Cool on a wire rack. Reduce the oven
   temperature to 350 degrees.
3. To make the filling, in the top of a double boiler over simmering
   water, melt the chocolate and shortening, stirring until smooth.
   Remove from the heat.
4. In a large bowl, using an electric mixer on medium speed, beat the
   condensed milk, eggs, hot water, almond extract, and salt until well
   blended. Beat in the chocolate mixture. Pour the mixture into the
   prepared crust and top with the pecan pieces.
5. Bake for 35 to 40 minutes, or until a cake tester inserted into the
   center comes out clean. Cool on a wire rack.
6. Whisk together the sugar and liqueur until smooth and lightly brush
   over the pecans.

LUSCIOUS CHOCOLATE ALMOND PIE

makes 8 to 10 servings

almond crust
1 cup all-purpose flour
1 cup chopped almonds
1 cup butter or margarine,
   softened
fluffy cream cheese filling
8 oz. cream cheese,
   at room temperature

1 cup powdered sugar
1 cup whipped topping
chocolate pudding filling
2 (3.4 oz.) packages
   chocolate pudding mix
2 cups cold milk
1½ cups whipped topping
½ cup chopped almonds

1. Position a rack in the center of the oven and preheat the oven to
   325 degrees.
2. To make the crust, in a medium bowl, combine the flour and almonds.
   Using a pastry blender or two knives scissor fashion, cut the butter
   into the flour. Press the mixture firmly onto the bottom and sides of
   a 9-inch glass pie plate.
3. Bake for 20 minutes. Cool completely on a wire rack.
4. To make the cream cheese filling, in a large bowl, using an electric
   mixer on medium speed, beat the cream cheese until smooth.
   Beat in the powdered sugar until smooth. On low speed, beat in the
   whipped topping. Spread evenly over the baked crust.
5. To make the chocolate filling, in a small bowl, using an electric mixer
   on high speed, beat the pudding mix and milk. Spread over the
   cream cheese filling. Chill for 1 hour. Fill a pastry bag with the
   whipped topping and pipe rosettes over the top of the pie.
   Serve chilled, sprinkled with the chopped almonds.

HOT FUDGE
SUNDAE PIE

makes 8 to 10 servings

Prepared chocolate cookie
crumb crust
1 quart strawberry ice cream,
softened
1½ cups hot fudge sauce
1 quart chocolate ice cream,
frozen

½ cup heavy cream
Maraschino cherries
Chocolate pieces
Chopped almonds

1. Bake the prepared pie crust.
2. To assemble, spread half of the strawberry ice cream over the crust
   and freeze for 30 minutes. Drizzle half of the fudge sauce over the
   top and spread with the remaining strawberry ice cream. Freeze for
   30 minutes.
3. Using a small ice cream scoop, arrange balls of the chocolate ice
   cream over the top of the strawberry layer. Drizzle the remaining
   fudge sauce over the top.
4. In a medium bowl, using an electric mixture on high speed,
   whip the cream until soft peaks form.
5. Fill a pastry bag fitted with a large star tip with the whipped cream.
   Pipe rosettes around the chocolate ice cream. Freeze for 30 minutes
   before serving. Garnish with the cherries and chocolate pieces.
   Sprinkle the almonds over the top.

MOCHA FUDGE PIE
WITH CHOCOLATE FILLING

makes 8 to 10 servings

mocha crust
1¾ cups all-purpose flour
⅓ cup Dutch processed
  cocoa powder
¼ cup granulated sugar
Pinch of salt
¾ cup butter or margarine
¼ cup cold strong brewed
  coffee
¼ cup coffee liqueur

mocha walnut filling
6 oz. semi-sweet chocolate,
  grated or finely chopped
6 oz. unsweetened chocolate,
  grated or finely chopped
2 tbsp. butter or margarine
⅔ cup granulated sugar
2 tbsp. buttermilk
2 tsp. coffee liqueur
½ cup ground walnuts
2 large eggs

1. Position a rack in the center of the oven and preheat the oven to
   350 degrees.
2. To make the crust, in a large bowl, combine the flour, cocoa powder,
   sugar, and salt. Using a pastry blender or two knives scissor fashion, cut in
   the butter to make a crumbly mixture. Stir in the coffee. If the mixture
   seems dry, add the liqueur, a tablespoon at a time. Press the mixture firmly
   into the bottom and sides of a 9-inch pie pan. Freeze until ready to fill.
3. To make the filling, in the top of a double boiler over simmering
   water, melt the chocolates and butter, stirring constantly until smooth.
   Remove from the heat. Stir in the sugar, buttermilk, liqueur, walnuts,
   and eggs and blend thoroughly. Pour into the prepared pie crust.
4. Bake for 35 to 40 minutes, or until a cake tester inserted into the
   center comes out clean. Cool completely on a wire rack.

AMARETTO
CHOCOLATE PUDDING

makes 4 to 6 servings

1 package (3.4 oz.) chocolate instant pudding mix
2 oz. semi-sweet chocolate, grated or finely chopped
1½ cups milk
2 tbsp. buttermilk
7 tbsp. amaretto

½ cup heavy cream
1 tbsp. granulated sugar
Sliced fresh peeled kiwifruit or strawberries for garnish
Macaroons for serving

1. In a medium saucepan, over low heat, combine the pudding mix, chocolate, milk, buttermilk and 6 tablespoons of the amaretto and stir constantly until the chocolate is melted and the mixture is smooth. Raise the heat to medium and cook, stirring constantly, until the mixture boils and thickens. Pour the mixture into 4 to 6 custard cups or ramekins.
2. In a medium bowl, using an electric mixer on high speed, beat the cream with the sugar and remaining 1 tablespoon amaretto until soft peaks form. Chill until ready to use.
3. To serve, place a dab of whipped cream on top of each cup of pudding and garnish with fresh fruit. Serve with macaroons on the side.

BAKED CHOCOLATE PUDDING

makes 6 to 8 servings

6 oz. unsweetened chocolate, grated or finely chopped
6 large eggs, separated
½ cup butter or margarine, at room temperature

1 cup powdered sugar
1 tsp. crème de cacao
5 tbsp. arrowroot or cornstarch
1 cup milk
1 cup heavy cream

1. Position a rack in the center of the oven and preheat the oven to 350 degrees. Lightly grease a 1½-quart casserole dish.
2. Melt the chocolate. Remove from the heat.
3. In a large bowl, using an electric mixer on high speed, beat the egg whites until stiff but not dry.
4. In another large bowl, using an electric mixer on medium speed, beat the butter and powdered sugar until fluffy. Beat in the crème de cacao. Beat in the egg yolks, one at a time, beating well after each addition. Pouring it in a steady stream, beat in the melted chocolate on low speed. Combine the arrowroot and milk and stir into the chocolate mixture. Stir in the cream. Fold in the egg whites. Pour the mixture into the prepared casserole dish.
5. Bake for 40 to 45 minutes, or until a cake tester inserted into the center comes out clean. Cool slightly and serve.

BARRIGA
DE FREIRA
makes 8 to 10 servings

1½ cups granulated sugar	3 large eggs
½ cup water	4 oz. unsweetened chocolate,
¾ cup finely ground almonds	grated or finely chopped
½ cup dried bread crumbs	1 cup milk or heavy cream

1. In a medium saucepan, over low heat, combine 1 cup of the sugar and the water. Cook, stirring occasionally, until the sugar is dissolved. Using a pastry brush dipped in cold water, wash down the sugar crystals on the side of the pan. Raise the heat to medium and bring to a boil. Cook, without stirring, for 2 minutes. Remove from the heat and immediately stir in the almonds and bread crumbs. Cover and let stand for 3 minutes.

2. In a medium bowl, using an electric mixer on medium speed, beat the eggs until thick and light-colored.

3. Stir the beaten eggs into the sugar mixture. Cook over medium heat, stirring constantly, until thickened. Do not allow the mixture to boil. Remove from the heat and transfer to serving bowl.

4. In the top of a double boiler over simmering water, melt the chocolate, stirring constantly until smooth. Stir in the milk and the remaining ½ cup sugar. Cook, stirring constantly, until smooth. Stir into the egg mixture. Cool to room temperature before serving.

BITTER-SWEET
CHOCOLATE MOUSSE
makes 4 to 6 servings

3 large eggs, separated
¾ cup plus 1 tbsp.
  powdered sugar
5 oz. unsweetened chocolate,
  grated or finely chopped

¼ cup butter or margarine,
  at room temperature
3 tbsp. raspberry liqueur
1 tsp. chocolate or vanilla extract
3 tbsp. strong brewed coffee
½ cup heavy cream

1. In a small bowl, using an electric mixer on high speed, beat the egg
   whites until stiff peaks form. Fold in 1 tablespoon of the powdered sugar.
2. Melt the chocolate. Remove from the heat and stir in the butter.
3. In the top of a double boiler, over simmering water blend the egg
   yolks, the remaining ¾ cup powdered sugar, the raspberry liqueur,
   and chocolate extract. Using a wire whisk, beat well until the mixture
   is thick. Place over simmering water and stir constantly for about 5
   minutes, or until the mixture is foamy. Remove from the heat. Blend
   the chocolate mixture into the egg yolk mixture. Beat in the coffee
   and cool for 5 minutes. Fold the egg whites into the mixture, stirring
   until completely blended.
4. In a small bowl, using an electric mixer on high speed, whip the cream
   until soft peaks form. Fold the whipped cream into the chocolate
   mixture. Spoon the mixture into 4 to 6 chilled custard cups or a chilled
   serving bowl. Chill for 4 hours, or until ready to serve.

Baking note: Due to the raw eggs in this recipe, it should be kept
refrigerated at all times, and for no longer than 1 week.

BLACK FOREST
PARFAITS

makes 4 to 6 servings

3 oz. cream cheese,
  at room temperature
2 cups minus 2 tbsp. milk
1 package (3.4 oz.) chocolate
  instant pudding mix
1½ tbsp. Kümmel liqueur
  or Aquavit

½ cup chocolate wafer
  cookie crumbs
1 can (21 oz.) cherry pie filling
Whipped cream for garnish
Ground hazelnuts for garnish

1. In a small bowl, using an electric mixer on medium speed, beat the
   cream cheese and ½ cup of the milk until smooth. Beat in the
   pudding mix and the remaining milk. Add the liqueur and beat for
   2 minutes.
2. Spoon half of the mixture evenly into 4 to 6 chilled parfait glasses.
   Sprinkle with chocolate wafer crumbs and cover with the pie filling.
   Top with the remaining pudding and chill for 30 minutes, or until
   ready to serve. Garnish with whipped cream and sprinkle with
   ground hazelnuts.

BLENDER
CHOCOLATE MOUSSE

makes 4 servings

1 large egg
1 envelope unflavored gelatin
1 tbsp. cornstarch
  or arrowroot
1 tbsp. cold water
1 cup boiling water
2 tbsp. mocha-flavored
  instant coffee powder

½ cup ricotta cheese
½ cup skim milk, chilled
2 tbsp. Dutch processed
  cocoa powder
½ cup granulated sugar
⅛ tsp. salt

1. In the container of a blender, combine the egg, gelatin, cornstarch, and cold water. Blend for 20 seconds. Add the boiling water and blend for 30 seconds. Add the coffee powder, ricotta cheese, skim milk, cocoa powder, sugar, and salt, and blend for about a minute, or until smooth.
2. Pour into four chilled custard cups and chill overnight or until set.

Baking note: Due to the raw egg in this recipe, it should be kept refrigerated at all times, and for no longer than 3 days.

CHOCOLATE APPLE PUDDING

makes 12 to 16 servings

2 oz. semi-sweet chocolate, grated or finely chopped
2 cups granulated sugar
1 cup hot water
½ cup crème de cacao
2¼ cups all-purpose flour

2 tsp. baking powder
1 tsp. baking soda
1½ tsp. ground allspice
½ cup butter or margarine, at room temperature
4 cups chopped apples

1. Position a rack in the center of the oven and preheat the oven to 350 degrees. Lightly grease a 2½-quart casserole dish.

2. In the top of a double boiler over simmering water, melt the chocolate, stirring until smooth. Stir in 1 cup of the sugar, blending until dissolved. Remove from the heat and stir in the hot water and crème de cacao.

3. In a large bowl, combine the remaining 1 cup sugar, the flour, baking powder, baking soda, and allspice. Using a pastry blender or two knives scissor fashion, cut in the butter to make a crumbly mixture. Fold in the apples.

4. To assemble, spread ⅓ of the apple mixture onto the bottom of the prepared casserole. Pour ⅓ of the chocolate mixture over the top. Repeat with the remaining apple and chocolate mixtures, ending with the chocolate mixture. Carefully swirl a spoon through the layers until the apple mixture is just moistened.

5. Bake for 45 to 50 minutes, or until thickened.

Baking note: Coffee liqueur can be substituted for the crème de cacao.

CHOCOLATE
CHOCOLATE MOUSSE
makes 8 to 10 servings

3 oz. unsweetened chocolate,
  grated or finely chopped
⅓ cup crème de cacao
¾ cup granulated sugar
Pinch of salt
3 large egg yolks

2 cups heavy cream
1 tsp. chocolate or
  vanilla extract
Fresh mint sprigs for garnish
Sliced orange or peeled and
  sliced kiwifruit for garnish

1. In the top of a double boiler over simmering water, melt the
   chocolate, stirring until smooth. Stir in the crème de cacao. Add the
   sugar and salt and continue to cook, stirring constantly, until the
   sugar is dissolved and the mixture is smooth. Remove from the heat.
2. In a large bowl, using an electric mixer on medium speed, beat the
   egg yolks until thick and light-colored. Pouring it in a thin stream,
   beat in the chocolate mixture until well blended. Set aside to cool
   to room temperature.
3. In a large bowl, using an electric mixer on high speed, whip the
   cream and flavored extract until soft peaks form. Fold into the
   chocolate mixture and pour into a serving bowl. Cover and freeze
   for 3 to 4 hours or until ready to serve. Remove from the freezer
   30 minutes before serving. Garnish with fresh mint and slices of
   oranges or kiwifruits.

Baking note: Due to the raw egg in this recipe, it should be kept
refrigerated at all times, and for no longer than 3 days.

CHOCOLATE CUSTARD

makes 8 servings

3 oz. unsweetened chocolate, grated or finely chopped

3 oz. semi-sweet chocolate, grated or finely chopped

2 tbsp. butter or margarine

6 large eggs

½ cup granulated sugar

3⅓ cups milk

2 tsp. chocolate or vanilla extract

1. Position a rack in the center of the oven and preheat the oven to 350 degrees.

2. Combine the chocolates and butter in a 1½-quart casserole dish and heat in the oven for 3 to 5 minutes. Remove from the oven and stir until blended. Chill for 20 minutes, or until the mixture is just starting to set. Using a spatula, spread evenly over the bottom and sides of the casserole dish. Chill for 30 minutes.

3. In a large bowl, using an electric mixer on medium speed, beat the eggs until thick and light-colored. Add the sugar, milk, and flavored extract and beat until the sugar is completely dissolved. Pour the mixture into the chilled casserole. Place the casserole dish in a roasting pan on the oven rack. Pour boiling water into the pan until it comes halfway up the sides of the casserole dish.

4. Bake for 80 to 90 minutes, or until a cake tester inserted into the center comes out clean. Remove from the hot water and chill for 30 minutes, or until ready to serve.

CHOCOLATE LIQUEUR CREAM
makes 8 to 10 servings

4 oz. semi-sweet chocolate, grated or finely chopped
4 large eggs, separated
½ cup granulated sugar

½ cup heavy cream
4 tbsp. crème de cacao
Whipped cream for garnish

1. In the top of a double boiler over simmering water, melt the chocolate, stirring until smooth. Remove from the heat.
2. In a large bowl, using an electric mixer on medium speed, beat the egg yolks until thick and light-colored. Beat in ¼ cup of the sugar. Beat in the melted chocolate, blending until no streaks appear. Beat in the cream. Return the mixture to the double boiler and cook over low heat until the mixture has thickened slightly. Remove from the heat.
3. In a medium bowl, using an electric mixer on high speed, beat the egg whites until stiff but not dry. Beat in the remaining ¼ cup sugar. Fold into the chocolate mixture and fold in the crème de cacao. Cover and chill for at least 2 hours.
4. To serve, spoon into 8 to 10 dessert cups and garnish with whipped cream.

CHOCOLATE MOUSSE À L'ORANGE

makes 8 to 10 servings

8 oz. semi-sweet chocolate, grated or finely chopped
3 tbsp. marshmallow creme
2 tbsp. thawed frozen orange juice concentrate

4 large eggs, separated
½ tsp. cream of tartar
Whipped cream for garnish
Grated orange zest for garnish

1. In the top of a double boiler over simmering water, melt the chocolate, stirring constantly until smooth. Add the marshmallow creme and orange juice concentrate, stirring until blended and smooth. Remove from the heat.
2. In a large bowl, using an electric mixer on high speed, beat the egg whites until foamy. Add the cream of tartar and continue beating until stiff peaks form.
3. In a small bowl, using an electric mixer on high speed, beat the egg yolks until thick and light-colored. Beat in the chocolate mixture. Gently fold into the egg whites, blending thoroughly. Spoon the mixture into 8 to 10 custard cups or ramekins and chill for 8 to 10 hours before serving. Just before serving top with whipped cream and sprinkle with grated orange zest.

Baking note: The mousse can also be chilled in a 9 or 10-inch serving bowl. Due to the raw eggs in this recipe, it should be kept refrigerated at all times, and for no longer than 3 days.

CHOCOLATE RASPBERRY SOUFFLÉ

makes 6 servings

1 cup fresh raspberries
2 tbsp. granulated sugar
1 envelope unflavored gelatin
¼ cup boiling water
2 large egg whites
1 jar (7 oz.) marshmallow
  creme

1 cup heavy cream
2 oz. semi-sweet chocolate,
  grated or finely chopped
½ cup whole fresh raspberries
  for garnish

1. Wrap a strip of aluminum foil or parchment paper around the top of a 3-cup soufflé dish so that it extends 2 inches above the rim and tie securely with string.
2. In a small bowl, mash the raspberries. Strain through a sieve into another bowl. Stir in the sugar and let stand for at least 10 minutes.
3. In a cup, sprinkle the gelatin over boiling water and stir until dissolved. Stir into the raspberries and chill until thickened but not set.
4. In a medium bowl, using an electric mixer on high speed, beat the egg whites until soft peaks form. Gradually add the marshmallow creme, a little at a time, beating until stiff peaks form. Fold the raspberry mixture into the egg whites.
5. In a large bowl, using an electric mixer on high speed, beat the cream until soft peaks form. Fold into the raspberry mixture. Fold in the grated chocolate. Pour the mixture into the prepared soufflé dish and chill 30 minutes, or until firm.
6. To serve, remove soufflé from the dish. Remove the foil strip. Transfer onto a serving plate and garnish with fresh raspberries.

EASY CHOCOLATE
MOUSSE

makes 8 to 10 servings

12 oz. semi-sweet chocolate, grated or finely chopped

**5 large eggs, separated
2 cups heavy cream**

1. Melt the chocolate. Remove from the heat and cool to room temperature.
2. In a large bowl, using an electric mixer on high speed, beat the egg whites until stiff but not dry.
3. In a medium bowl, using an electric mixer on medium speed, beat the egg yolks until thick and light-colored.
4. In another medium bowl, using an electric mixer on high speed, whip the cream until soft peaks form.
5. Beat the chocolate into the egg yolks until smooth and yellow streaks no longer appear. Fold ⅓ of the egg whites into the chocolate mixture. Fold the chocolate mixture back into the remaining egg whites until streaks no longer appear. Fold in the whipped cream. Spoon the mousse into a large glass serving bowl. Cover and chill for 1 to 2 hours, or until ready to serve.

Baking note: Due to the raw eggs in this recipe, it should be kept refrigerated at all times, and for no longer than 3 days.

GRAND MARNIER MOUSSE

makes 6 to 8 servings

1 cup heavy cream
¼ cup granulated sugar
½ cup fresh orange juice,
  strained

8 oz. semi-sweet chocolate,
  grated or finely chopped
3 large egg yolks
¼ cup Grand Marnier

1. In a medium bowl, using an electric mixer on high speed, whip the cream until soft peaks form.
2. In the top of a double boiler over simmering water, warm the sugar and orange juice. Add the chocolate and stir constantly until it is melted and smooth. Remove from the heat.
3. In a medium bowl, using an electric mixer on medium speed, beat the egg yolks until thick and light-colored. Pouring it in a thin stream, beat in the chocolate mixture on low speed. Fold in the whipped cream and Grand Marnier. Pour into a serving bowl and chill for at least 2 hours, or until ready to serve.

Baking note: Due to the raw eggs in this recipe, it should be kept refrigerated at all times, and for no longer than 3 days.

POTS AU CHOCOLAT

makes 6 to 8 servings

6 oz. semi-sweet chocolate, grated or finely chopped
¼ cup water

1 tbsp. butter or margarine
3 large eggs, separated
¼ cup cherry liqueur

1. In the top of a double boiler over simmering water, melt the chocolate with the water, stirring until smooth. Remove from the heat and beat in the butter. Using an electric mixer on medium speed, beat in the egg yolks and liqueur.

2. In a medium bowl, using an electric mixer on high speed, beat the egg whites until stiff but not dry. Fold into the chocolate mixture. Pour into 6 to 8 chilled custard cups and chill overnight.

Baking note: Due to the raw eggs used in this recipe, it should be kept refrigerated at all times, and for no longer than 3 days.

SPICED CHOCOLATE BREAD PUDDING

makes 6 servings

2½ cups heavy cream
2 oz. semi-sweet chocolate,
   grated or finely chopped
2 tbsp. butter or margarine
2 large eggs
3 tbsp. coffee liqueur
1 cup soft white bread,
   cut into ½-inch cubes

⅔ cup granulated sugar
½ tsp. ground cinnamon
¼ tsp. ground nutmeg
Pinch of salt
2 tsp. chocolate extract

1. Position a rack in the center of the oven and preheat the oven to
   325 degrees. Lightly grease and sugar a 1-quart soufflé dish or
   casserole dish.
2. In a large saucepan, over medium heat, heat the cream until bubbles
   start to form around the sides of the pan. Add the chocolate and
   butter, stirring constantly, until melted and smooth. Remove from the
   heat and cool.
3. In a small bowl, using an electric mixer on medium speed, beat the
   eggs until thick and light-colored. Beat in the liqueur.
4. In a large bowl, combine the bread cubes, sugar, cinnamon,
   nutmeg, and salt. Using a wooden spoon, stir in the cream mixture.
   Add the chocolate extract. Stir in the egg mixture and pour into the
   prepared baking dish and spread evenly.
5. Bake for 65 to 70 minutes, or until a cake tester inserted into the
   center comes out clean.

BANANA CHOCOLATE CHIP MUFFINS

makes 12 muffins

1¾ cups plus 2 tbsp.
  all-purpose flour
⅓ cup granulated sugar
2 tbsp. Dutch processed
  unsweetened cocoa powder
1 tbsp. baking powder

1 cup mashed bananas
  (2 medium)
⅔ cup canola oil
1 large egg, beaten
1 cup semi-sweet
  chocolate chips

1. Position a rack in the center of the oven and preheat the oven to
   425 degrees. Line twelve 2¾-inch muffin cups with paper baking cups.
2. In a large bowl, combine the flour, sugar, cocoa powder, and
   baking powder.
3. Blend the bananas, oil, and egg into the dry ingredients, mixing just
   until blended. Fold in the chocolate chips. Spoon the batter into the
   prepared muffin cups, filling them ¾ full.
4. Bake for 15 to 20 minutes, or until a cake tester inserted into the
   center comes out clean. Cool in the muffins cups on a wire rack
   for several minutes. Invert onto the rack to cool completely.

BRUNCH
COFFEE RING

makes 10 to 12 servings

coffee cake
2 cups all-purpose flour
1 tsp. baking powder
1 tsp. baking soda
½ tsp. salt
1 cup sour cream
1 cup granulated sugar
2 large eggs
1 tsp. Praline liqueur
½ cup semi-sweet
chocolate chips

topping
½ cup all-purpose flour
½ cup packed light
brown sugar
1½ tsp. Dutch processed
cocoa powder
¼ cup butter or margarine,
at room temperature
½ cup walnuts or pecans,
chopped

1. Position a rack in the center of the oven and preheat the oven to 350 degrees. Lightly grease a 9-inch tube pan.
2. To make the cake, combine the flour, baking powder, baking soda, and salt.
3. In a large bowl, using an electric mixer on medium speed, beat the sour cream, sugar, eggs, and liqueur until combined. Gradually blend in the dry ingredients. Fold in the chocolate chips. Pour the mixture into the prepared pan and spread evenly.
4. To make the topping, in a medium bowl, combine the flour, brown sugar, and cocoa powder. Using a pastry blender or two knives scissor fashion, cut in the butter to form a crumbly mixture. Blend in the walnuts. Crumble the mixture over the batter in the pan.
5. Bake for 1 hour to 65 minutes, or until a cake tester inserted into the center comes out clean. Cool in the pan on a wire rack.

CHOCOLATE BREAKFAST CAKE WITH CHOCOLATE SAUCE

makes 10 to 12 servings

2½ cups all-purpose flour
1½ cups granulated sugar
1 tbsp. active dry yeast
1 tsp. baking soda
½ tsp. salt
2 oz. unsweetened chocolate, grated or finely chopped

1 cup butter or margarine
1 cup milk
¼ cup Dutch processed cocoa powder
3 large eggs
1 cup chocolate sauce
¼ cup sliced almonds for garnish

1. Position a rack in the center of the oven and preheat the oven to 350 degrees. Lightly grease and flour a 10-inch Bundt pan.
2. Combine the flour, sugar, yeast, baking soda, and salt.
3. In the top of a double boiler over simmering water, melt the chocolate and butter, stirring until smooth. Stir in the milk and cocoa powder until smooth. Remove from the heat.
4. In a large bowl, using an electric mixer, beat the eggs until thick and light-colored. Pouring it in a thin stream, beat in the chocolate mixture. Gradually blend in the dry ingredients just until blended. Pour into the prepared pan. Cover with a towel and let rise for 2 hours, or until an indentation is left in the dough when poked.
5. Bake for 40 to 45 minutes, or until a cake tester inserted into the center comes out clean. Cool in the pan on a wire rack for 15 minutes. Invert onto a serving dish. Drizzle chocolate sauce over the top of the cake, allowing it to drip down the sides, and sprinkle with sliced almonds. Serve warm.

CHOCOLATE CHERRY PECAN MUFFINS

makes 12 muffins

2 cups all-purpose flour
½ cup granulated sugar
1 cup chocolate chips
1 cup chopped dried cherries
½ cup chopped pecans
1 tbsp. baking powder
½ tsp. salt

1 cup milk
⅓ cup canola oil
⅓ cup butter or margarine, melted
1 large egg
12 whole pitted cherries, (canned)

1. Position a rack in the center of the oven and preheat the oven to 400 degrees. Lightly grease twelve 2¾-inch muffin cups.
2. Combine the flour, sugar, chocolate chips, cherries, pecans, baking powder, and salt.
3. In a large bowl, using an electric mixer on high speed, beat the milk, oil, butter, and egg for 2 to 3 minutes, until smooth. Gradually blend in the dry ingredients, mixing just until incorporated. Spoon the batter into the prepared cups, filling them ¾ full. Press 1 whole cherry into the center of each muffin.
4. Bake for 20 to 25 minutes, or until a cake tester inserted into the center comes out clean. Cool in the muffin cups on a wire rack for several minutes. Invert onto the rack to cool completely.

CHOCOLATE CHIP MUFFINS

makes 12 muffins

1 large egg
2 tbsp. butter or margarine, melted
¼ cup granulated sugar
2 oz. semi-sweet chocolate, grated or finely chopped

⅓ cup plus 1 tbsp. all-purpose flour
Pinch of salt

1. Position a rack in the center of the oven and preheat the oven to 375 degrees. Line twelve 2¾-inch muffin cups with paper baking cups.
2. In a medium bowl, using an electric mixer on medium speed, beat the egg until thick and light-colored. Beat in butter and sugar. Add the chocolate, flour, and salt and blend just until moistened. Spoon the batter into the prepared muffin cups, filling them ¾ full.
3. Bake for 18 to 20 minutes, or until a cake tester inserted into the center comes out clean. Cool in the muffin cups on a wire rack for several minutes. Invert onto the rack to cool completely.

CHOCOLATE CHIP ZUCCHINI BREAD

makes 2 loaves

2 cups all-purpose flour
1 package (3.4 oz.) instant chocolate pudding mix
1 cup semi-sweet chocolate chips
½ cup shredded coconut
½ cup almonds, chopped
1 tsp. baking powder
1 tsp. ground cinnamon
1 tsp. ground allspice
½ tsp. salt
3 large eggs
1 cup granulated sugar
½ cup packed light brown sugar
1 cup canola oil
1 tbsp. orange liqueur
2 cups grated zucchini
Powdered sugar for garnish

1. Position a rack in the center of the oven and preheat the oven to 350 degrees. Lightly grease and flour two 9 by 5-inch loaf pans.
2. Combine the flour, pudding mix, chocolate chips, coconut, almonds, baking powder, cinnamon, allspice, and salt.
3. In a large bowl, using an electric mixer on medium speed, beat the eggs until thick and light-colored. Beat in the sugars. Beat in the oil and liqueur. Beat in the zucchini. Gradually blend in the dry ingredients. Divide the mixture between the prepared pans and spread evenly.
4. Bake for 55 minutes to 1 hour, or until a cake tester inserted into the center comes out clean. Cool in the pans on a wire rack. Remove from the pans and place on a serving plate. Sprinkle with powdered sugar.

CHOCOLATE GINGERBREAD

makes 12 to 15 servings

2 cups all-purpose flour
2 tsp. baking powder
¼ tsp. baking soda
2 tsp. ground cinnamon
1 tsp. ground ginger
¼ tsp. salt
1½ oz. unsweetened
   chocolate, grated or
   finely chopped

⅓ cup vegetable shortening
2 large eggs
¼ cup granulated sugar
¼ cup packed light
   brown sugar
¼ cup dark molasses
½ cup milk
Powdered sugar for garnish

1. Position a rack in the center of the oven and preheat the oven
   to 350 degrees. Lightly grease a 13 by 9-inch baking pan.
2. Combine the flour, baking powder, baking soda, cinnamon, ginger,
   and salt.
3. In the top of a double boiler over simmering water, melt the
   chocolate and shortening, stirring until smooth. Remove from the
   heat. Beat in the eggs, one at a time. Beat in the sugars. Beat in the
   molasses and milk. Gradually blend in the dry ingredients. Pour the
   mixture into the prepared pan and spread evenly.
4. Bake for 20 to 25 minutes, or until a cake tester inserted into the
   center comes out clean. Cool in the pan on a wire rack. Remove from
   the pan and place on a serving plate. Sprinkle with powdered sugar
   and cut into squares.

DOUBLE CHOCOLATE MUFFINS

makes 12 muffins

2 cups all-purpose flour	1 tbsp. baking powder
1½ cups miniature chocolate chips	½ cup vegetable shortening
¾ cup Dutch processed cocoa powder	1 cup granulated sugar
	1 large egg
	1 cup milk

1. Position a rack in the center of the oven and preheat the oven to 400 degrees. Lightly grease twelve 2¾-inch muffin cups.
2. Combine the flour, chocolate chips, cocoa powder, and baking powder.
3. In a large bowl, using an electric mixer on medium speed, beat the shortening and sugar until fluffy. Beat in the egg. Beat in the milk. Blend in the dry ingredients, stirring until just moistened. Spoon the batter into the prepared muffin cups, filling them ¾ full.
4. Bake for 18 to 20 minutes, or until a cake tester inserted into the center comes out clean. Cool in the muffin cups on a wire rack for several minutes. Invert onto the rack to cool completely.